EXTREME PLACES

The
Longest
Bridge

Other books in the Extreme Places series include:

EXTREME PLACES

The
Longest
Bridge

Darv Johnson

**KIDHAVEN
PRESS™**

THOMSON

™

GALE

San Diego • Detroit • New York • San Francisco • Cleveland
New Haven, Conn. • Waterville, Maine • London • Munich

LIBRARY OF CONGRESS CATALOGING-IN-PUBLICATION DATA

Johnson, Darv, 1971–
   The longest bridge / by Darv Johnson.
      p. cm. — (Extreme places)
Includes bibliographical references and index.
   Summary: Explains the purpose, design, construction, and costs of the Akashi Kaikyo Bridge in Japan.
      ISBN 0-7377-1416-6
   1. Akashi Kaikyo Ohashi (Kobe-shi), Japan)—History—Juvenile literature.
[1. Akashi Kaikyo Bridge (Kobe-shi), Japan) 2. Bridges—Japan.] I. Title. II. Series.
   TG106.K63K64 2003
   624'.5'0952—dc21

                                                                 2002010655

Contents

Measuring the Longest Bridge

The gap separating the islands of Honshū and Awaji in Japan is more than two miles wide, and the water there is cold, swift, and deep. On its surface, more than a thousand ships of all sizes hurry by every day. This is the setting for the world's longest bridge.

The Akashi Kaikyo Bridge links the two islands by leaping that band of water, known as the Akashi Strait. The bridge travels 2.5 miles in all, a distance it covers in three great spans.

A **span** is the distance a bridge travels between supports. The longer the span, the more challenging and expensive the bridge is to build. That is why the longest bridges in the world are ranked according to their spans, and not to their total length. It is also why the Akashi Kaikyo is the world's longest.

Both of the bridge's outer spans are an impressive, although not record-breaking, 3,150 feet long. But its central span stretches out 6,529 feet, or about 1¼ miles. A jogger would have to sweat through five laps on an average running track to cover the same distance.

The Akashi Kaikyo's central span is almost a quarter mile longer than that of its closest competitor, the Store-Baelt Bridge in Denmark. Although the two bridges are separated by thousands of miles, their designs have much in common. Like all of the world's longest bridges, they are both suspension bridges.

A Tried and True Design

Suspension bridges can reach great lengths because their design allows them to carry tremendous weight. In bridges

The Akashi Kaikyo Bridge spans a greater distance than any other bridge in the world.

of this type, the roadway that cars travel on is suspended, or hung, by cables from two giant main cables overhead.

The main cables, in turn, are draped over two tall towers sunk deep into the bed of the river, lake, or sea. The Akashi Kaikyo's towers soar as high as ninety-story skyscrapers, which means that the world's longest bridge is also the world's tallest. Cars crossing the six-lane bridge are suspended more than three hundred feet above the water at the halfway point.

The long concrete and steel roadway pulls down hard on a suspension bridge's main cables. To keep the bridge from collapsing, the main cables are fastened to the shore at each end into solid concrete or rock **anchorages**.

Stretching Out

Modern suspension bridges are built longer as the cables that hold them up are made of stronger materials. The cables in the earliest suspension bridges were made of grass twisted together. In the Himalayas, pathways were suspended from ropes thrown across chasms. Even today in remote parts of India, travelers cross gaps of more than six hundred feet on crude suspension bridges made of bamboo ropes.

Later, bridge builders began to use iron chains. The earliest major bridge of this type was the Union Bridge that connects Scotland and England. Built in 1820, the bridge still stands. Later in the nineteenth century, builders turned to dozens of steel wires twisted together to form thick cables. This is still the standard for modern suspension bridges.

A mountain climber crosses a bridge made from willow twigs in the Himalayas.

The Brooklyn Bridge is the oldest bridge built with steel-wired cables. Completed in 1883, the famous bridge links the boroughs of Manhattan and Brooklyn in New York City. A central span of 1,594 feet made it the longest bridge of its day by far. But bridges have come a long way in the last century. It would take four such spans, laid end to end, to match the length of the Akashi Kaikyo's central span.

The familiar, bright orange Golden Gate Bridge in San Francisco, with a central span of 4,200 feet, became the world's longest bridge when it opened in 1937. Almost three decades later, the Verrazanno Narrows Bridge in New York earned the title with a longest span of 4,620 feet traveling between two 690-foot-tall towers. The Verrazanno Narrows is still America's longest bridge, but it has fallen to sixth in the world, far behind the Akashi Kaikyo.

The Best of the Rest

Suspension bridges are not the only long bridges in the world. Other bridge designs can also reach extreme lengths.

Cable-stayed bridges look a lot like suspension bridges. The way they work, however, is completely different. In a suspension bridge, the main cables run over the towers. This helps to distribute the weight to the anchorages on the shore. The cables in a cable-stayed bridge are attached to the towers, which bear the load alone.

The longest cable-stayed bridge in the world is also in Japan, not far from the Akashi Kaikyo. The Tatara Bridge relies on a central span of 2,920 feet to cross the waters between the Ikuchi and Omishima Islands.

The arch bridge, another common design, has great natural strength. Its graceful arches carry the weight of the

The majestic Golden Gate Bridge rises high above San Francisco Bay.

An arch bridge spans a serene river dotted with boats.

roadway to the supports at either end. The 1,700-foot bridge at New River Gorge, West Virginia, is the world's longest arch bridge. Hanging 876 feet above the river, this bridge is also one of the world's highest.

The Beam Bridge

The simplest design is the beam bridge. It has a horizontal surface with a vertical support at each end to bear the load. The earliest bridges made by humans—trees chopped down to span a stream or river—were a crude form of a beam bridge. Today, beam bridges are often used on roads and highways because they are relatively easy and inexpensive to build.

The spans of beam bridges are rarely more than a few hundred feet long. If they were longer than that, they would collapse under their own weight. The Lake Pontchartrain Causeway, for example, stretches for almost twenty-four miles across a Louisiana lake. But to cover this distance, it relies on about fifteen hundred individual

Cars travel along the Lake Pontchartrain Causeway in Louisiana.

spans. Each span has an average length of one hundred feet. This is a fraction of the length of the Akashi Kaikyo Bridge's central span. For this reason, the Lake Pontchartrain Causeway does not make the list of the world's longest bridges.

The Akashi Kaikyo is not the world's longest just because its designers wanted to win a contest, however. It is the longest because the conditions and the setting demand it.

Planning the Akashi Kaikyo

Japan is a bridge builder's paradise. The nation is made up of a long string of islands stretching for fifteen hundred miles through the Pacific Ocean. All that water means many opportunities to bring places and people together by building bridges.

For decades the Japanese government wanted to link its four main islands—Honshū, Shikoku, Hokkaidō and Kyūshū—through a network of bridges and tunnels. The hope was that easy travel between the islands would bring business and tourists to places that had been hard to reach before. That way, wealth and jobs could spread throughout the country.

Japan turned the idea into reality one step at a time. Honshū and Kyūshū were joined by three undersea tunnels and a suspension bridge. Honshū was linked to Hokkaidō, meanwhile, by one of the world's longest railroad tunnels.

The Final Connection

The final piece in the puzzle was a connection between Honshū, the largest island, and Shikoku, the smallest. Shikoku is one of the poorest and least developed areas of Japan, largely because of its remote location across the Seto Inland Sea. Few tourists made the long journey to the island's pine-covered mountains, small fishing villages, and shrines.

Without a bridge, tourists and residents alike had to cross between the two islands by a forty-minute ferry ride. This presented a problem when, for example, residents fell ill and needed to seek medical treatment in Kōbe. They

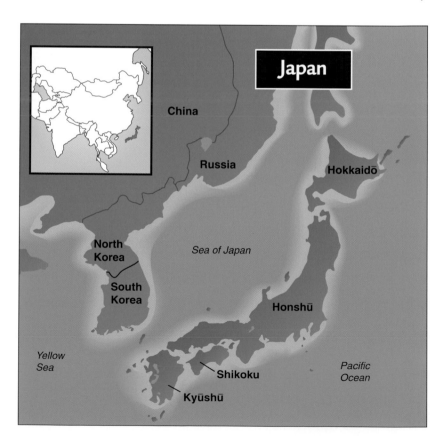

might have to wait hours for the next ferry to arrive. In bad weather, the ferries did not run at all. With a bridge connecting the two islands, the trip would take just three minutes, rain or shine.

Two bridges were needed to make the connection between Honshū and Shikoku. One bridge would connect Shikoku to the small island of Awaji, which lay in between. A second bridge—a very long bridge—would run from the other end of Awaji across the Akashi Strait to Honshū.

An Impossible Dream

This second bridge, which would later be named the Akashi Kaikyo, was first proposed by a Japanese politician in 1914. At the time, the idea was dismissed by another politician from Shikoku. He called it an impossible dream.

For decades, the critic was right. The Japanese economy was not yet strong enough to take on such an expensive project, and it did not have the technology to build such a long bridge.

World War II brought more delays. After the destruction from the war, the country had to focus on rebuilding what it had lost instead of creating grand new projects. But gradually Japan grew stronger and the bridge was built.

In 1970 the Honshū-Shikoku Bridge Authority was established to link the two islands. The bridge authority planned three different routes, each featuring a series of bridges. Some would be long cable-stayed bridges, while others would be suspension bridges. The biggest of them all was the Akashi Kaikyo, the longest suspension bridge the world had ever seen.

Workers board electric cars during the construction of Japan's Seikan Rail Tunnel, which links the Honshū and Hokkaidō islands.

The Right Bridge for the Job

Picking the right kind of bridge for the setting was not easy. The Akashi Kaikyo project commanded the attention of some four hundred **engineers**, specially trained workers who design bridges, buildings, and roads.

The engineers had many factors to consider. The bridge had to be wide enough to handle the estimated thirty-seven thousand cars that would travel on it every day. It had to be strong enough to survive high winds and high enough to allow the biggest ships to pass under it.

Most important, the bridge had to be long enough to leap a two-mile body of water without ever blocking it. The Akashi Strait, which connects Ōsaka Bay and the Seto Inland Sea, is very important to fishing and commerce in Japan. Some fourteen hundred ships sail through it every day, loaded down with valuable cargos. Those ships could

Designers for the Akashi Kaikyo project realized that many boats of different sizes would have to pass under the bridge daily.

not afford to be slowed down by a bridge's towers. Nor could they run the risk of accidentally striking one.

Different bridge designs could do some of these jobs. Moveable bridges, modern versions of the drawbridges in medieval castles, could swing up out of way of passing ships. Simple beam bridges could easily cover the distance. And these kinds of bridges had their advantages. They were cheaper and easier to build because of their

A moveable bridge opens to allow tall ships to pass through.

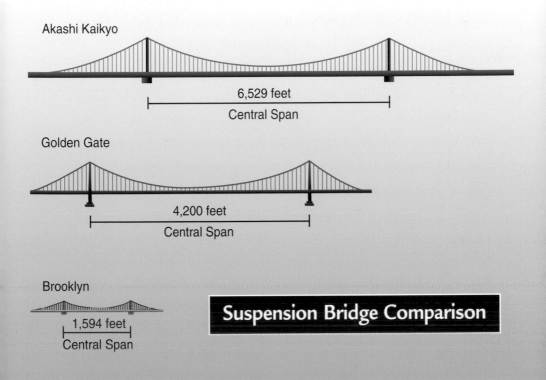

Akashi Kaikyo

6,529 feet
Central Span

Golden Gate

4,200 feet
Central Span

Brooklyn

1,594 feet
Central Span

Suspension Bridge Comparison

shorter spans. They were also less likely to sway in the wind or take a tumble in an earthquake.

Only one design could go far enough and high enough to meet all the demands of the Akashi Strait, however, and that was a suspension bridge. After years of careful study, the engineers announced plans for a suspension bridge. The main towers were to be separated by 6,529 feet. This way the towers would be safely outside of the shipping channel. They would also be far enough apart to make the Akashi Kaikyo the longest bridge in the world.

A Bridge Too Far?

The bridge plan had its critics. Some people noted that fewer than one thousand cars a day used the ferry to cross the Akashi Strait. They wondered if such a big bridge was needed to carry the small amount of traffic.

Others worried about the bridge's cost. Estimates started at $4 billion and climbed steeply from there. Cars and trucks would have to pay a toll to cross the bridge, but that would cover only a small part of the bill. Tax money would be used for the rest, and the government would still be paying for the bridge fifty years after it was built. Critics believed that the money could be put to better use elsewhere.

None of these concerns was enough stop the progress of the Akashi Kaikyo Bridge. In 1988 the builders went to work.

Under Construction

Planning the Akashi Kaikyo was a difficult task, but building it was even tougher. The project took ten years, thousands of workers, and billions of dollars.

Construction began in 1998 at the bottom of the Akashi Strait. There, engineers took samples of the seabed where the two towers were to be placed. They wanted to be sure that the ground there was stable enough to support the bridge's great weight.

Next, machines on floating barges started to dig. Their job was to reach down through the water and remove mud and gravel from the seabed, so that the towers could sit on solid rock.

While the digging was underway, two **caissons** were under construction at local shipyards. Caissons are bottomless, double-walled steel cylinders that serve as molds for the concrete foundations. Each one is 262 feet around and 230 feet tall.

Though the caissons were taller than twenty-story buildings, they were designed to float. Tugboats—twelve per caisson—towed them across the Akashi Strait to their final destinations. The caisson walls were filled with water to sink them to the bottom of the sea. The job was done with such precision that the giant structures struck the bottom less than an inch from their intended targets.

Caissons are not sealed with steel at the bottom. Instead the sea bed serves as the floor. Rocks and gravel must

A caisson machine spews solid clay from the ground below at a Middlesborough, England construction site.

be cleared out of the compartment before construction can continue.

Caisson Disease

The workers who built the first big suspension bridges faced great danger when performing this task inside caissons some eighty feet below the water's surface. Caisson disease, or the bends, crippled dozens of men during the construction of the Brooklyn Bridge in the nineteenth century. The pressure of being so deep released nitrogen bubbles into their blood. The bubbles blocked oxygen's passage through the veins, causing painful cramps and even paralysis. Some compared it to having a heart attack in different parts of the body.

Fortunately, the Akashi Kaikyo builders spent almost all their time above the water's surface. They used remote-controlled equipment to do difficult and dangerous tasks such as clearing rocks and debris out of the caissons. Thus, they avoided many of the risks of working deep underwater.

Cementing the Job

After the caissons sank into position, a barge on the surface mixed a special type of concrete that does not dissolve in water. The concrete poured into each caisson for three days and nights until they were full.

The builders then surrounded the concrete foundations with a circle of giant rocks, each weighing more than a ton. The rocks block the strong underwater current, which otherwise would wash away mud and gravel and

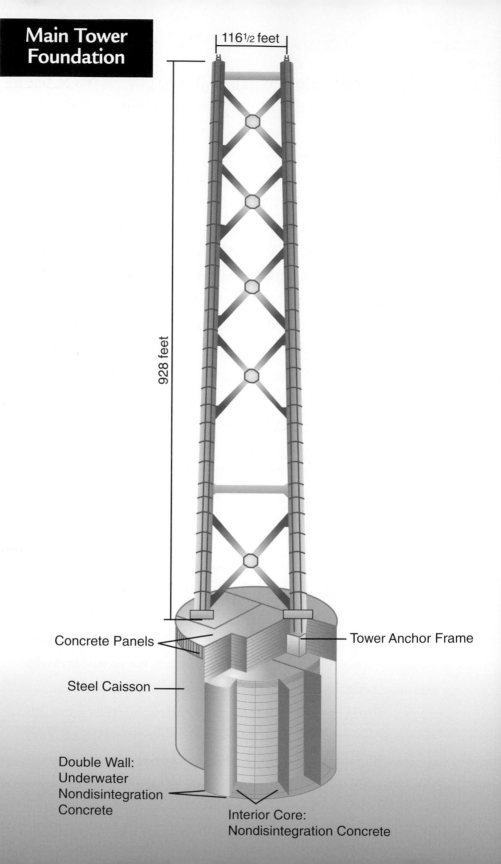

Main Tower Foundation

116 1/2 feet

928 feet

Concrete Panels

Tower Anchor Frame

Steel Caisson

Double Wall:
Underwater
Nondisintegration
Concrete

Interior Core:
Nondisintegration Concrete

make the foundations unstable. After a year of work, the foundations were ready to support the main towers.

Going Up

As the foundations went up underwater, the towers came together on land. Each tower was built in thirty-foot sections at a factory. The steel blocks were taken by barge to the bridge site. They were then stacked one on top of the other until the towers reached their full 928-foot heights.

A special crane did the heavy lifting. The crane set one block in place and then pulled itself up to the next level. From there it reached down to hoist another block into position.

Building each piece of the bridge required great precision. The towers, for example, had to stand up perfectly straight to do their jobs properly. The tops could not lean more than 2.5 inches away from vertical. That is about the length of a well-used pencil.

Throwing a Rope

Soaring up straight as arrows, the towers were ready to carry the weight of the cables by 1993. The cable-laying process began with the placement of the pilot ropes. Pilot ropes are temporary cables that travel from one anchorage to the other over the tops of the main towers. They make it easier to set the permanent cables in place.

On most bridge-building projects, the pilot ropes are dragged across the water by boat. But because the builders of the Akashi Kaikyo could not interrupt traffic in the busy shipping lane, they took to the air. A helicopter hoisted the

A worker walks the cables of the Brooklyn Bridge.

ropes and draped them over the towers. It was the first time that a helicopter had been used to lay pilot wire.

Workers built **catwalks** alongside the pilot rope. These narrow walkways, high in the sky, made it possible for them to put the main cables in place.

Miles and Miles of Wire

The world's longest bridge would need the world's strongest cables to hold it up. At a factory, 127 high-strength steel wires were pressed together to form a strand. Then, 290 of these strands were bundled to

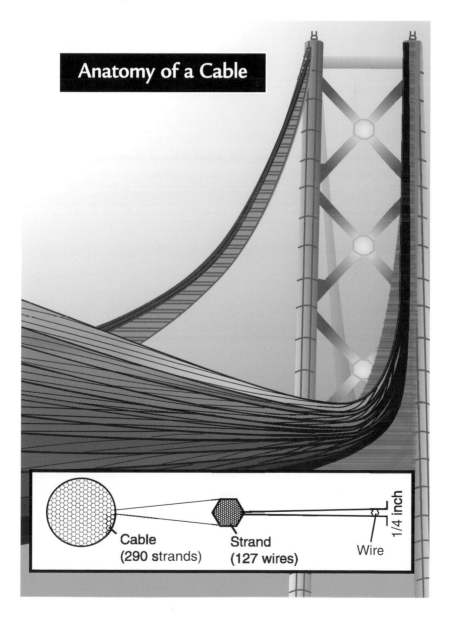

Anatomy of a Cable

Cable
(290 strands)

Strand
(127 wires)

Wire

1/4 inch

form a single cable. Each cable is almost four feet around. In all, they contain enough wire to circle the globe more than seven times. The cables were secured to the shore by tremendous concrete foundations, or anchorages.

From the main cables, the workers hung dozens of smaller cables that support the weight of the suspended roadway. The cables were carefully adjusted so that each carried equal weight.

Finishing Touches

The final step was the construction of the **truss**, a steel frame that supports the roadway. A floating crane lifted football field–length sections of the truss into position at each end of the bridge. Smaller truss pieces were rolled out over the part of the bridge that had already been built, and then they were bolted on. The two ends of the bridge met in the middle in June 1995. Workers began to pave the road, paint the steel, and add the electrical wires to light the bridge. The job was almost done.

Safety was a big concern of the Akashi Kaikyo builders. In a huge construction project such as this one, hazards lurked everywhere. Workers could slip and fall from high in the bridge cables, or be crushed by a piece of equipment. Remarkably, there were no fatal accidents in the ten-year-long construction of the Japanese bridge.

Open for Business

The world's longest bridge was finally finished on April 5, 1998. Buddhist priests and the crown prince and princess

Trusses can be seen on the underside of the Golden Gate Bridge.

of Japan were there to mark the occasion. A spectacular fireworks display lit up the sky in celebration. Then, with the snip of a ceremonial ribbon, the bridge opened for business. Cars and trucks filled its six lanes.

More than five thousand cars crossed the Akashi Kaikyo in its first hour of operation. The people of Japan had waited a long time to use this bridge.

A Bridge Built to Last

Engineers knew the Akashi Kaikyo Bridge would have to be strong. The bridge had to be able to support its own weight, which builders call the **dead load**. It had to hold up the weight of the **live load**—all the cars, trucks, and people that would cross it. And that was not all.

The Akashi Kaikyo also had to be tough enough to survive natural disasters. In the area where the bridge was built, two types of natural disasters have occurred.

The region is famous for its **typhoons**. These are giant storms much like the hurricanes that strike parts of the United States. These storms could bring swirling winds of up to 180 miles per hour. When these winds whipped through the Akashi Strait, the giant bridge, with its long, exposed span, had to be ready for them.

More danger would come from underground. Like the rest of Japan, the Akashi Kaikyo is located right in the middle of an earthquake zone, where cracks in the earth's crust can cause violent shocks. The Akashi Kaikyo had to be strong enough to survive tremors of up to 8.5 on the **Richter scale**, which measures an earthquake's force. The bridge designers estimated that an earthquake that powerful would occur only once every 150 years.

Into the Wind

Engineers planned carefully for all this moving and shaking. First, they built a detailed model of the bridge. Though the model was just one-hundreth the size of the actual bridge, it was still 130 feet long. Then they placed the model in a **wind tunnel**. A wind tunnel allows engineers

Astronaut candidates visit an enormous NASA wind tunnel. Engineers use tunnels like these to determine how much a bridge will sway in the wind.

to test how air affects aircraft, buildings, and other objects. They blasted the model bridge with wind from all angles to test its strength and stability.

The Lessons of Galloping Gertie

Bridge builders had learned about the dangers of the wind the hard way. The slender twenty-eight-hundred-foot Tacoma Narrow Bridge opened in Washington State in 1940. But its designers had failed to make the bridge deck strong enough to withstand the wind. Four months later, the bridge collapsed in a relatively weak forty-two-mile-per-hour wind.

A motion picture taken at the time shows the twistings and turnings of the bridge before it dropped into the water. Its wild movements earned it the nickname "Galloping Gertie."

Fins and Pendulums

The designers of the Akashi Kaikyo took great care to avoid such a catastrophe. One of the safety features they added to their bridge is called a vertical stabilizer. A series of vertical plates, which look like the tail fins on airplanes, hang beneath the bridge deck. When the wind blows, they reduce vibrations by balancing the air pressure above and below the decks.

The Akashi Kaikyo has another unusual feature to make it even more stable. Twenty giant **pendulums**, similar to the ones that swing back and forth in grandfather clocks, were built into the bridge's towers and deck. The ten-ton globes are suspended from above and can move in any direction.

A section of the Tacoma Narrow Bridge crashes into Puget Sound on November 7, 1940.

When winds or an earthquake push the bridge one way, the pendulums move the other way. By shifting their heavy weight around, they help the bridge keep its balance.

The bridge's main towers, meanwhile, are both very strong and very flexible. They are designed to bend—rather than break—with the motion of the cables they support. With all these safety features in place, engineers

The Kōbe earthquake was so strong that it toppled parts of the Kōbe -
Osaka freeway in 1995.

believed that the Akashi Kaikyo was tough enough to survive almost any natural disaster.

The Kōbe Earthquake

They did not have to wait long to find out if they were right.
The bridge faced its first test before it was even finished. In
January 1995, an earthquake measuring 7.2 on the Richter

scale struck near the bridge, The quake killed five thousand people and destroyed one hundred thousand buildings in the nearby city of Kōbe. It twisted highways and cracked railroad tracks. It also opened a new fault, or crack in the earth, that could be seen from the bridge less than two miles away.

A Bit of a Stretch

Construction was halted for a month while engineers searched for damage to the bridge. Despite the destruction all around, they found that the bridge had stretched only a little. The earthquake moved the tower and anchorage on the Awaji side a few feet farther away. As a result, the world's longest bridge became 2.6 feet longer than its original design. After a few adjustments, construction quickly resumed to make up for the new length.

The Kōbe earthquake relieved some of the stresses underground, making another big quake unlikely in the near future. After passing its first test, bridge builders believe the Akashi Kaikyo will remain in use for centuries. After all, the Brooklyn Bridge is still carrying the load almost 130 years after it opened to traffic.

Challenges on the Horizon

How long the Akashi Kaikyo will remain the longest bridge in the world is a harder question to answer. Already, several bridges have been planned that would be far longer than the current record holder.

Some of those bridges would join continents together. Europe and Africa are separated by only 8.5 miles at the

Strait of Gibraltar. One engineer has proposed to bridge this gap with four mighty spans, each one far longer than the Akashi Kaikyo's longest. If the bridge is ever built, the trip from Spain to Morocco would become just a short drive.

Another planned bridge would cross over the Strait of Messina to link the island of Sicily with the rest of Italy. The central span of this bridge would be about two miles

A bridge may one day span the Strait of Gibraltar (pictured), connecting Spain and Morocco.

The Brooklyn Bridge has carried traffic for more than a century.

long. This is almost twice as long as the Akashi Kaikyo. The bridge deck would be nearly two hundred feet wide. This is nearly twice as wide as the previous record holder. The width would allow the bridge to support two railroad tracks and ten different roads.

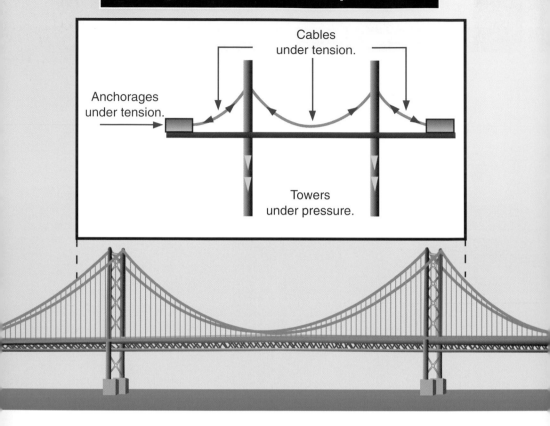

These projects would challenge the engineers who design the world's long bridges. They would also test the governments that pay for them. Construction on the Strait of Messina Bridge is scheduled to begin in 2004, but many experts believe that the project is too expensive for Italy to build. It is likely that Akashi Kaikyo will remain the world's longest bridge for years to come.

Glossary

anchorages: Concrete foundations that secure a bridge's main cables to the land.

caissons: Watertight enclosures inside which the foundations for a bridge's towers are built.

catwalks: Narrow, elevated walkways.

dead load: A bridge's weight, without traffic on it.

engineers: Specialists in the construction and operation of bridges, buildings, roads, or airfields.

live load: The weight of all cars, trucks, and other traffic that a bridge must support.

pendulums: Bodies hung from a fixed point that swing back and forth freely.

Richter scale: A device that measures the strength of an earthquake.

span: The distance a bridge travels between supports.

truss: A rigid steel frame that supports the roadway of a bridge.

typhoons: Violent tropical storms.

wind tunnel: A chamber for testing the effects of wind on bridges, airplanes, and other machines.

For Further Exploration

Book

David J. Brown, *Bridges*. New York: Macmillan, 1993. The book describes the world's great bridges from Roman times to the present. Includes many color photographs.

Periodicals

Satoshi Kashima and Makoto Kitagawa, "The Longest Suspension Bridge," *Scientific American*, December 1997. As part of an issue dedicated to the world's biggest structures, the authors describe the construction of the Akashi Kaikyo Bridge.

Dennis Normile and Frank Vizard, "A Bridge So Far," *Popular Science*, March 1998. A detailed look in words, photographs, and illustrations at the world's longest bridge.

Websites

Akashi Kaikyo Bridge (www.hsba.go.jp). The official website of the world's longest bridge includes information on its construction and history.

Bridge Basics (www.matsuo-bridge.co.jp). The site describes the six basic bridge designs with graphics and statistics on the longest of each type.

Building Big: All About Bridges (www.pbs.org). An introduction to the world's great bridges and the people who build them. Includes information on the Akashi Kaikyo. It also includes a section that allows students to plan and build different bridge designs.

Index

Picture Credits

About the Author

Darv Johnson is a writer who lives in New Orleans. He has previously written about the Amazon rain forest and about Ronald Reagan for Lucent Books.